The Radical Pulsivity of Life

The Radical Pulsivity of Life
Poems of Attentiveness

Elijah Byrd Deyton

FOREWORD BY
Claire E. Wolfteich

RESOURCE *Publications* • Eugene, Oregon

THE RADICAL PULSIVITY OF LIFE
Poems of Attentiveness

Copyright © 2025 Elijah Byrd Deyton. All rights reserved. Except for brief quotations in critical publications or reviews, no part of this book may be reproduced in any manner without prior written permission from the publisher. Write: Permissions, Wipf and Stock Publishers, 199 W. 8th Ave., Suite 3, Eugene, OR 97401.

Resource Publications
An Imprint of Wipf and Stock Publishers
199 W. 8th Ave., Suite 3
Eugene, OR 97401

www.wipfandstock.com

PAPERBACK ISBN: 979-8-3852-4728-8
HARDCOVER ISBN: 979-8-3852-4729-5
EBOOK ISBN: 979-8-3852-4730-1

VERSION NUMBER 07/30/25

I dedicate this work to my grandmother, my Mammaw, my Nanagene, Dianna Margene Ottinger. As this work began, she took up a horrific struggle with cancer, and her persevering presence in spirit and voice became a font of great grace, hope, and joy for the words that occupy these coming pages. Her life bears witness to our collective call to attentiveness and solidarity.

Contents

Foreword by Claire E. Wolfteich | ix
Acknowledgements | xi
Introduction: A Note On Theology | xiii

Attentive to the Spirit: Spiritual Poems

    A Poem About Walking | 2

    Time and Repetition | 3

    A Note On The Call | 4

    Reflections on the Clock | 6

    Apocalyptic Fervor: Hurry, Hurry | 7

    Gardening | 8

    To the God of Saints | 11

    Triptych I: Holy Saturday | 13

    Carve me, Paint me, Cast me | 14

    Triptych II: Crucifixion | 16

    Forget the Unforgettable | 17

    Triptych III: Resurrection | 18

    The Fissure of Mystery | 19

    The Shock of Indifference | 20

    Thinking Kites | 22

    Where Do We Go?!? | 23

    Cosmo-Play: A Not-So-Subtle Foray! | 25

Attentive to God: Prayers

    Prayer: Iconize | 28

    Prayer: Should It Not Arrive | 29

    Prayer: Easter | 30

    Prayer: It Didn't Arrive | 31

Attentive to the Domestic: Familial Poems

    On the Child | 34

    The Chance of Life | 35

    What's In A Name? | 36

    Rufus Wingo Deyton | 37

    Charlotte Marie Deyton | 39

    Edgar Byrd Deyton | 41

    Saoirse Ruth Deyton | 43

    Jungle Gym Hands | 45

    Grin | 48

    To My Carlee (I'll Make the Toast) | 49

Foreword

This book of poetry calls us to attention. From his experience of chronic illness, Elijah Deyton makes visible the repetitive contours of everyday life and the spiritual insights and struggles that course through them. These poems bare open his experiences of illness, conversion, love, longing, and deep hope. The poet wrestles with bodily fragility and humiliation, retreat and fear. He is closely aware of death and time: the clock "tick- tocking", "Hurry hurry!" in one poem, time "precious" and "fleeting." Sickness "interrupts"—breaking speech, writing, and rhythms of everyday life. Illness forces him to attention. What he comes to notice is the most radical truth and call of his life. While infused with a deep spirituality, the poems do not express an easy faith. Faith is wrestled out of him, at a cost, and he often simply does not "see the way." Yet he longs deeply for God to mold him into a worthy image and he assents to God's creative shaping. These poems speak beautifully to vocation, for the "God of the saints" is calling through all the realness of life, and whether we know it or not, he writes, we are "already responding to this call." For Eli, love is woven into that call. The final section sings of family love, what has sustained him and continues to call him in a new season of life. Recently married, he writes of his love for Carlee and dreams of the children they might have, giving them names and envisioning them with playful detail.

    I first encountered Eli Deyton's poetry when he took a course I was teaching on spiritual autobiography. His poems flowed, full of piercing intelligence, longing, and faith. Poetry seemed the form of writing most capable of witness to a God who surpasses all language. His words do indeed witness, pointing to a Life that pulses in the midst of the everyday, calling us to notice and turn.

—Claire E. Wolfteich

Acknowledgements

A huge thank you to the Boston University School of Theology, particularly to the Center for Practical Theology's 'Creative Callings' grant project. Without their financial support, this work would not be possible. I also wish to thank a few individuals. Thank you to Claire Wolfteich and many of my fellow seminarians at the Boston University School of Theology. Without your encouragement, this work would have never seen print. Thank you to Brian Robinette; over many meals and office chats, you have pointed me to peace of spirit and mind. This work is a direct product of our time together, and I cannot thank you enough for your friendship and mentorship. Thank you to Bryan Stone for our many conversations discussing the open, process, and relational theolgies that undergird this work; his encouragement of both my identity as a theologian and writer have proven invaluable. Thank you to my mother and father, Heidi and John Deyton, as well as my mother-in-law and father-in-law, Dana and Charlie Campbell. Your incessant support and love granted me the ability to write and think, a privilege so few have these days. Lastly, thank you to my patient and passionate wife, Carlee. You have and will continue to be my pride and joy; I love you, and I still must confess—as I do to you everyday—that my life would be impossible without you.

Introduction: A Note On Theology

To fall ill is to know both the adoration and disgust of repetition. First, adoration: repetition is one's gasping expression of love; it is a commitment to living a shared life. Shared with friendly objects and feelings, with one's neighbors, the always ready-to-hand cleaning supplies, groceries, etc., and what's more, with the persons, who without, chores, patterns, and intentions would be lacking; abruptly missing their referent, their object of love.

Next, disgust: I pace and fold, pace and put away. Laundry piles up, dishes pile up, inhibitions pile up. . . over there, on the other side of the room in the corner, their shadow casts doubt upon what little time I have left in the day to think and write, and secure enough hope from moment to moment. All this falls again to the same line of thought, to the same time that is fraught with disgusting repetitions. And yet, it was only when I fell ill that I cherished both my hatred and love of these endless, blurring repetitions.

There is Life inside of life; a clandestine living, separate, but still infusing the purely visible and ordered world. That is where the self resides, where you keep all your secrets and opinions, where you roll up your sleeves and do that dirty, most intimate job of thinking and pleading and hoping, where it all gets carried out—carried away. And it is here, where repetitions are fed upon, for without the automatic hourly rendition of responsibility, one's mind could not be free to wander off into eternity, or even just today. And yet, most do not pause and thank the ceaseless task of living life, so that Life may be held, but rather, they rarely thank anything or anyone in those ceaseless moments of repetition.

Only illness reveals the begging, the pleading, the resignation of the heart that would do anything for just one more day of only worrying about those tedious, thankless repetitions. For it is when these repetitions are disrupted, carried out with the most irregular, undependable feeling of instability granted by the knowledge that my flesh or your flesh is corrupted, torn asunder, that we come to realize the mundane pulsivity of our radically open lives. We may die, we may live, we may cry, we may carry on. We *may*. The forgettable becomes unforgettable for us. But what does any of this have to do with theology?

Theology is the mystic-poetic native tongue of the panting, dying creature. And yet, from whence does this creature's suffering come? I write from a disabled and uncooperative body that often limits and prevents me from acting in the world. I must also note that I have inherited this body from a mother who has suffered from similar illnesses since my birth. My experience with disruption has always been shared in community. As such, my illness, her illness, the illness of every other that I have encountered in text or person, grants me that which often escapes many, namely, attention.

In my chronic illness, I am arrested often by just the slightest disruption to the sensing of that clandestine Life; in these disruptions, I have learned to read the signs of the flesh, the very sighs of my nervous system. And in that lesson, I have learned to give attention to the other, to the world, to every creature and everything; not necessarily always with my gaze, not always with my mind or with my body, but rather in feeling. Solidarity is a felt sensation of one's self meeting and coming to cherish that which is encountered in its quiddity, in its what makes it whatness. I am in solidarity with this world, with this grand becoming, in the clandestine feeling of a sigh, in the groaning of expectation from within the bones and dust of all that must suffer and learn to love change.

We owe our dawn to a trace—a whispering absence—which beckons even now to us from our origin unto our destiny. Theology is the form of attention that places this trace into focus; the native tongue of the panting, dying creature is the tongue that issues a response to this trace. And yet, always this tongue is reduced; reduced to either political statecraft, propositional logic, or, worst of all, to that which offers certain solutions; rather, the tongue I am describing is a troubling, trying two-edged sword that always destabilizes and reveals new questions and new problems which makes all that exists reduced to that sigh which grounds the ever becoming truth of clandestine Life.

Theology is the discourse of the impossible revelation of the trace from within the feeling of myself as the feeling of the pulsivity of the grandeur of Life. In a simple phrase, then, theology is the gentle opening of the heart to cherish and attend to all that *is, was, and will be–come* to this Life of mine; a gentle paying attention to suffering, hope, the imagined, the real, and all the somewhere-in-between(s). What a gift of grace and charity is that which has made me come to see this! Join me in gazing at and lingering with the subsequent maze of spiritual, theological, and mundane images, emotions, ideas, phrases, and events that emerge from my encounter with the radical pulsivity of Life.

Attentive to the Spirit: Spiritual Poems

A Poem About Walking

Pitter-patter pavement constructed out of intentions.
She caresses her curled, frizzy tresses.
"How?" she wonders, "could I be more truly me?"
She misses the glance of that which others within from without.
Consciousness ruptures in the infinite excess of the *in–between*—
But, alas, pitter-patter pavement remains merely the case.

Shod shorn and lacking what is noble,
He crosses the pitter-patter of her thoughtful, mental rambles.
Intentionality shifts to masculine countenance.
This encounter is what renders us sane—what remains in
    the overflow of infinite excess.
Tend to the left, and our she misses our he,
In the pitter-patter flow of steps upon pavement.

Time and Repetition

There is a morning, bald and bitterly cold.
Its shadows long; its precipice lofty,
Because you must tell the truth.
But fear not!
For dawn's light is near.
Life is here in tension found,
So journey onward, dissonance bound.

There is a midday sun that ensnares your bones.
Fragility is written on your flesh with the burns of heat
    only harsh labor knows.
Weak-minded, yet? Feeble-hearted?
The Host of Heaven has barely even started.

There is a night, marvelously dark,
He comes to execute your pride.
In private, he summons you.
Without public witness, you die.
Unto yourself, you moan, and weep, and sigh.
And as existence would have it, again, you will rise.

A Note On The Call

We had a punch-down,
Drag-out night again didn't we . . .
Me and You . . .

And it's funny how you skip time,
Journey across the minefield of my mind,
And drag me back here, back there, rather,

To the smell of putrid flesh,
The indecency of nail-pierced wrists.

It's funny (well, maybe not)
How a face can offer something to share,
An invitation to co-inhere.

To give and receive life from another . . .
Well, you get it, you, hanging *there*, hanging *out*.
And it's oh so sad,
Humiliation remains the only way to teach me that.

But anyway,
We had a knock-down, drag-out
Fit again, didn't we?

Like a retreating boxer, ripped and battered,
I make my way on back toward the showers,
Tail between my legs and knowing I'm a bit of a coward.

And as that stream of steam pours forth,
Prayers bleating,
I bleeding,
Recall the shame of even daring a back and forth.

Your Yes, my no.
And yet, I Know your Yes is a Yes for all, forever . . .
I am caught back up in that Yes
Which tore your life from your bones,
Which carried forth a promise,
And a promise, and another promise,
Which tears by, at, and through me,
As if I were being stoned.

Yes, that Yes, which has only ever gently prodded.
What a shame, I, a violent creature,
Would choose such rage, such ferocity,
In response to your gentle,
breath-full, calmest call.

My dearest, truest, gentle friend,
I guess You win,
Till we meet again,
For another all-out, punch-down
Drag-out brawl.

Reflections on the Clock

"Hello, Master."
This yielding salutation is oft whispered by the eyes.
Our gaze speaks, admits, confesses . . .
Much more than our own voices.

Reflections on the clock.
The play is double;
For you, my master, are both the measure and command.
Work is guided and issued by your return of my gaze.

Master, your hands grasp me, arrest me, direct me.
Ticking compulsively, you inflict me with the movement of your dial.
Reflecting on the clock is my *reflection on the clock*, composed under the imposition of limits From your tick-tock.
The play is double.

Apocalyptic Fervor: Hurry, Hurry

Hurry, Hurry!

Come and cast your vote.

For this Universe's fate

Falls upon your momentary, barely sparking hopes!

Grace be damned,

Righteous hate be chaste;

Let us all be given over to abysmal, pointless outrage!

For Halcyon calls

And Elysium gapes,

Torn open, violated by our hands, our eyes, our tastes.

But all this mysteriously is veiled and unveiled in the sparing space of a moment's notice.

The voice that has authored time and place has called you to speak to your lack of faith.

The trace streaks across the night sky, and apocalyptic spears dance and hide.

And we, we the people below the stars and above the dead,

We are left to worry and dread the query which we always have:

Who on Earth is to be fed?

Gardening

When's the last time
You bandaged your blisters and callouses,
Hid the abuse of a spade or hoe?

Yeah, me too.

And so while gardening is a mere memory for me,
At the moment at least,
Let me invite you to take hold of this seedling;
We have much planting to do, and much to discuss
About these recent earth-groans.

God is mulch; God is a weed.
I'll say more, but for a moment,
I must remind you that this means
You must learn to slow down and re-breathe.

God is mulch.
Without them, we can not seed,
Not fully, anyhow,
And not in the best way.
Without mulch,
Our soil suffers from a lack of care.

Nutrients, protection, and stability.
Mulch is a shield and guarantor of care.
Mulch also unifies,
It ensures that the soil and plant
Are mutually brought together.
As the thinkers and blabbers would have it,
To *perichoretically co-inhere.*

Life is webbed together across a plane of mulch.
God is mulch,
And it snuffs out weeds.

And yet,
God is a weed.
From the bottom of your nicely
Pampered flower bed,
Something wickedly wild this way comes,
Breaks the stable-layered beauty of the mulch,
Is powered by that radiant Sun above,
And then,
God is a weed, just as God is mulch,
And all we can see is one side of either case at a time,
But God is the flower bed,
The weed,
The mulch,
Dynamic grace and holy restraint.
Hell, God is even there,
At this very garden's entry gate.

And all we can muster is a part for the whole,
Because we often see no value in either mulch or the weed,
But, there they are, just the same.
God is unificatory pleasure in protective structure,
And that which must break through those layers of stricture.

An antinomy which animates all *Animal symbolicum*
(To borrow Cassirer's phrase).
Creation breathing in, breathing out,
Positing up until the moment of negation;
And what's more?

This dynamicity is so grand and frustrating,
We often give up trying to comprehend or demonstrate,
That beauty which greets us in every soil-soaked plot
    of provisional place.

But oh, how we forget, myself included,
That gardening is an awareness
Of balance, reciprocity, unbridled hope, and moments of
   unbearable restraint.

Garden more often,
In your heart, mind, and soul,
For every other that we encounter
Will sure be glad to know,
You take seriously all the hard work and effort that is
   required to grow
In the garden(s) of God.

To the God of Saints

Batten the hatches,
Secure the hopes of your children,
Death beckons on and on and on . . .

And oh, how the bittersweet notes
Of a wuthering soundscape
Lash the ears of those who desire charity.

Pray all yee who hear, to the God of saints.
May He carry on, with our help, despite the carrion
That one day all will awaken at the sound
Of the trumpet,
Because we heeded Christ's clarion call.

Pray all who be,
To the God of saints,
That no longer sins will you be captive to;
And yet, even then, the Lord has plans that will convict and subvert the derision we have all wrought
So that souls may be saved, and hearts, in love, may be sought.

And precious is the time that you call fleeting,
Let eternity mock, and ridicule, and decry
what you so completely forgot and dream not;

For the God of the saints has held out for all
And you, us, we, despite our lack,
Whether we know or not,
Are already responding to this call.

Triptych I: Holy Saturday

It is Holy Saturday, even though it is Tuesday in March,
Some two thousand years after the rupture of time.
It is Holy Saturday, and the violence left in the wake of the trace
    is most intimately known to us.

Lord, I do not see the way.
Lord, I do not see the way.
Blood runs o'er these lands,
And it seems the shackles of history and shame bind my hands.

It is Holy Saturday and I do not see the way.
And, Lord, I am not sure You do.
Yet, I stand and do not move.
For if this impossible is to become,
Then what am I to do or say? . . .

Lord, in the startling streak of your trace,
I simply must confess I do not see the way.

Carve me, Paint me, Cast me

Carve me, Paint me, Cast me;
Call me, Trust me, Make me.
This is the incessant demand of a love that serves.
A love that finds its call in the voiceless trace of the beloved.

My bones ache with a blazing arthralgia.
Burdened by nostalgia,
Of times I did not make myself your total vessel.

Oh! the trauma, the formidable task of contorting myself
   to your reflection,
Your iconic reference, a footnoted flesh.
Alas, not my hands but thine Lord!
Again, I see myself as the sole god, and my will as the ticking cosmos
   that exclusively manages existence's toil.
But what spoils, recall now my soul that I am the tree and you,
   Lord, the ground.
I am the canyon, and you Lord that mighty aquatic serpent:
   Carve my flesh.
I will hold still while the master sketches.
Tend to my shape, notice my shades.
Tenderly represent, Lord, what You tenderly prepared from
   the hidden foundation of the world.
Stain me, Lord, put your flesh on my bones, render your life
   in my corpse: Paint my flesh.

And when all this is done, throw me in your melting bronze
 my Lord to preserve your work.

I will take the refining fire; I will eagerly bear the torrid flames.

For to be preserved in your form, Oh Lord is now my only aim:
 Cast my flesh.

Triptych II: Crucifixion

To have flesh,
To put on, to take up, to be keenly aware of this *here* flesh,
Is to risk rejection.

The Cross, as well as the Christian life following in its wake,
Was, is, and will be, an acceptance of this risk.
The incarnation, that trace which scars and bleeds into our hearts and minds, history and culture, even now,
Was an act of risk.

And how do we respond? We hung God, Christ, our victim,
Upon a tree to suffocate and hemorrhage all hope.
"Eloi, Eloi, lama sabachthani?"
The crucifixion, our reduction, our rejection, of this *here* holy flesh.

Forget the Unforgettable

Sickness interrupts a life like it does this line . . .

And then the rhythm of becoming bounces back in your favor.
  One more moment to forget the unforgettable, so to speak.

But let me not dwell or stop here,

Instead, I turn to think, to thank Sister Infirm.

For without her touch, I might begin to think I am finished.

I may begin to forget how to pray,

How to live.

I may forget the unforgettable; that death will come sometime,
  someday.

But let me reside here, in a moment of peace, knowing that
  to die well, is to die knowing that on my own, I am incomplete.

Let me recall the forgotten, back before the unforgettable.

When sickness could not wrest from me another letter, line, or dot.

There in that time before measure, in that space before shape,

That is where the forgotten will become once more truly
  unforgettable for me.

Triptych III: Resurrection

Arise! The light from which there is no return has shone forth!
Flesh *ahead-of-the-world* revealed in the breaking of bread;
This is how Christ, *messiah*, comes.

And what's more, me and you, creation expressed in one accord,
Shall be as he was!
Shall know the end of death.
History, time, regret . . . will come to know that infinite breath.

And this my soul bears in mind,
As my hands and feet lose themselves in time,
As my mind tends to the love of this *here* life,
Yes, my soul will contemplate that respite:
The resurrection of *my* body, and the advent of eternity's full
   attendance in *my* life.

The Fissure of Mystery

The fissure of mystery is thrice upon me:
Hatred. Renunciation. Despair.
And all this, Christ crucified, risen, ascended.
Read with a slant instead of a curve, and then a split me
  becomes split we.

All because I desire Your flesh, the mystery of mysteries poured out;
I have turned my back on a culture that cannot taste or eat.

But no.
I have not revolved or dismissed, or loosened my love,
My hope, my service.
I have bonded myself to that body that makes many into one.
And here I am drawn to see:
What can only be a mystery,
They have claimed it as their own understanding.

Possession is 9/10's of *their* law,
And where does that leave a poor man in search of grace like me?

No, I with Francis, and Clare, and Lawrence, and Elijah, and
  Cecilia, and Augustine, and those Cappadocian, Victorine,
  Jesuit, Dominican, and Benedictine fiends . . .
No, I cast my lot with them, for what may sustain the beauty,
  truth, and goodness of their fruit Must sustain me.
All this to say, the body broken upon a tree,
Resurrected and returned just for me,
That is who, what, and how I choose to be . . . to eat.

The Shock of Indifference

The shock of indifference is a dull, subtle pain.
It gently slides in like a knife; except not at all,
when one ponders faith, or food, or rain.

You see it's much more silent, much more. . . nothing.
It doesn't even resemble shame.
Nor the sense of shame that accompanies all sin,
all derision, all blame.

It is nothing,
No thought,
No hatred or embrace.
It is absence without any presence to negate.

And that is why no God can we, the people of my age,
Taste or Smell or Feel or Fear or Rejoice In or Love
Or Care or Declare or Confess or Question or Address.
Sensing the trace requires an awareness of Life,
A sense of presence that reveals a lack.

We negate the space for even lack to appear,
For empty cross-examinations,
For the opening of pure communication.

Our symbols, our words, are reduced to nothing,
Because for them to have meaning,
There would need to be a gap
For which something could stand.

The shock of indifference reveals this much,
The words I type, the thoughts you have thunk,
Are worth nothing, because the distance that my mind must travel across space and time
To unfold an idea, to send an invitation to your mind,
All have no means of transport.
For the distance, the space, and the time, lack any meaning without recourse
To a space, a trace, a concern to desire.

The shock of indifference is that it feels like nothing,
Because it is nothing,
Because it would never allow a feeling,
which would require an ultimate concern.
Desire is blind.
Hope is blind.
Knowledge is blind.
Indifference is blind.

Here, in this wasteland, there is hidden a horizon,
But for those who have become victims
Of the shock of indifference,
Hidden it remains.

Thinking Kites

The thinking kites, how they trap me in their dance.
No need to romanticize . . . except there is.
For the ground burdens even the freest dreams,
And the sky remains one's only true horizon.
Yes, thinking kites, they may breathe an air of bliss,
They may bear the marks of hope, and, yes, thinking kites,
That's all there needs to be.
No bliss or hope is real on its own.
That's why thinking kites, requires one to think in kites,
To dream in spite, to set fire, to blaze the summer setting sky alight.
Yes, to dare to catch the wind,
In the open face of my dearest friend and kin.
Thinking kites require a prayer, a dream,
And a brave mind to dare and believe
That one idea might catch flight.

And now, we see,
Those of us tossed into the sea of history,
We may be drowning, but what beauty there is, at least to me;
To drown, surrounded by a sky full of thinking kites,
What wondrous possibilities.

Where Do We Go?!?

Time must be made incarnate;
But how? By place, where time and space meet to form a whole,
 a moment.
And yet, my *here*, my place, has evaporated.
And so, to whom do I address these next few lines?
Where do we go when the light that discerns light and darkness
 is nowhere to be found?

I am seeking here in the *no-place*.
Much like the liturgy itself,
History, *my history*, has been in-broken;
Eternity among us already has begun,
The Absolute made personal,
That is what You gently reassure me.

Yes–You!
A person, who I am irrevocably shattered by, that *no-place*
Has become Divine Face, illuminated by that light,
That light which discerns the light and the dark,
That original light, which beckons creation to come,
Which harkens work to be done,
Which is the envy of the Sun...
No, the perfection of that stupendous star.
As what has been prefigured is succeeded and fulfilled,
So our Sun is perfected in the Son;
That divine wisdom, which always was, is, and shall be.
The Sun becomes Son, when I enter the *no-place*.

But what of *this* place, this space and time rendered embodied?
It is full of suffering and many become bereft,
There are lies and deceit, both spiritual and of flesh,
There is hate and regret;
And yet, the eye of faith tells of a different set.

A gentle gaze, reserved for those who can see Being not just as,
But can see beyond to Becoming which is delightful and felicitous.
Creation, Life, and Death; all these become what they are
Only in the Light that discerns light from dark,
Vice from virtue,
Meaning from intentionlessness,
Hope from disinterest,
Safety from plight,
And, bliss from fright.

Where do we go?!?
When we have lost all our faith, our place, our subtle hold
    on that primeval trace?
I do not know for you, but I go to the *no-place*,
Where Eternity illuminates via the Light which turns my gaze
    from despise to delight,
Where the Sun has become Son,
And light and darkness may be seen for what they truly are.
I go to the *no-place*, and I invite you to come;
For it is here that time receives its space, the Spirit incarnated
    gifted to us.

Cosmo-Play: A Not-So-Subtle Foray!

Yes; that which springs from the edge of this sticky, dynamic Life
    is a whispering dart;
Silent then seized we are!
And being seized we lie in the moment-to-moment gaps
    in space-time,
We do what creation beckons forth: we play!

The risk of Life all for the endeavor of gardening desire,
Growing up vinery, like blue-blooded veins,
And patches of green finery-like eyes of bright piercing sheen.

This mystery which grants itself the ability to be heard and seen,
Yes, that pulsating Life blisters us with its fervid heat.
Which causes chaotic derision unseen.
The trace of this mystery lingers hopelessly openly, terrorizing me.

But who has planted this trace in my garden?
This seed in my womb?
Who has beckoned forth such a lovingly, loveless wound?

Why Messiah has sprung up, sprung out, has come!
Leap, Skip, Desire, Become!

For the trace has given His name
So that I might choose to become that gift
From on high as has been given and hidden
In the blossoming bosom of this here Life.

I am because You who pervades via cosmo-play
Has come to invade and rapturously ravage me:
my heart, my mind, and my soul.

Attentive to God:
Prayers

Prayer: Iconize

In the name of the Father, and of the Son, and of the Holy Spirit:

My Lord and my God, pervade this world with your grace and your peace. Many in this world seek refuge, a love for themselves that will turn and reveal joy in the depths of their heart, the hope that resides, often dormant and not accessed in their flesh.

You, my Lord, are that refuge, that joy, and that hope. Make me more and more into an icon of Christ who reflects these fruits and many more in a world predominated by consumption, compression, and the worship of efficiency, always to the detriment of the value or recognition of persons.

To exist and resist, both have their genesis in the name of the Father, and of the Son, and of the Holy Spirit.

Prayer: Should It Not Arrive

My God, thank you for the proleptic vision offered in the resurrection of your Son, Jesus Christ. In Him, we see the past as we were made to be, the present as the selfless donation of our lives to all we encounter, and the future as reunion, communion, and perfection in our own resurrected flesh. Let this be my hope, my fuel, my passion, and my joy.

Let the culture of pressure, the world of necessity, demand something of me that only You may fulfill, so that I may, in asking You to fulfill the demands placed on me, be a witness to the Life given in You.

I pray for peace and goodwill, but should it not arrive on its own, I will give my body, my spirit, and my mind to ensure its presence. Only through your strength, through your grace, will my attempts be made whole; I pray that you make your Spirit known through me and my presence.

All this I ask for in the name of the Father, and of the Son, and of the Holy Spirit.

Prayer: Easter

Today, I will pray from below.

Easter is coming soon, and the Church is near.

We gather, metamorphosed.

Finitude has become my brother or sister, here among my brothers and sisters.

My hope is here in this community, seeking community with the originator of otherness.

Light, fruit, flesh.

All become intelligible and renewed in this space.

Easter, the transformation of death, the communal witness to gift.

To the Father of light, to the Son who has undergone the darkness of night, and to the Spirit that long-suffers our requests, I pray in Thy name: may peace come, may we enter resurrected being, and may we come to mirror the communal love at the very founding of the mystery.

Prayer: It Didn't Arrive

In the name of the Father, and the Son, and the Holy Spirit. Amen.

It didn't arrive . . . Something altogether new has. A seeming impossible, ever-possibility has come. And why would I be surprised, to be alive is to be inconceivable, and You are the God of all Life; the inevitable, ineffable pulsivity of mind and heart, soul and strength.

I prayed that you grant me what was needed to carry on, and you did. I am to be given the chance to hold your dearest, most mysterious hounds of the heavenly beauty: children.

How can I confess that which feels so complete in me and the world? I hold you dearly in my heart, and because of this, I am dearly held in yours.

In the name of the Father, and of the Son, and of the Holy Spirit. Amen.

Attentive to the Domestic:
Familial Poems

On the Child

Behind each child's eye,
There, glisten veiled and obscured,
is Incomprehensible vulnerability;
The Infinite spell, revealed in that gladening face.

And, as each age has often misplaced,
the child is our vision unto grace.
Forgotten till encountered,
Mistook until embraced,
Their vocation unto wisdom, wound, and wonder,
Is our very own.

All eternity is wrapped in the hands of a child,
Reaching out here and now,
In this very time and place.

The Chance of Life

The chance of Life is precious.
And the beauty of Hope is that it is allergic,
Allergic to predictions.
Be as Hope.

Embrace the absolute lack of certainty.
Knowing and knowledge only deal in death and impossibilities.

Dynamic grace, washed serene;
I am pleading with you,
Let the mystery be as it is seen.

For the chance of Life is precious,
far too precious for all our noise;
Be as Hope.

What's In A Name?

Well, certainly expectation!
No, not pressure or thoughtless commitment to a form,
Or type, or end (in the teleological sense).

Anticipation, rather, like the awaiting of the arrival of a friend,
The newness of a bride's gentle beaming pride,
Or even, just in the moment-to-moment grace,
Encountered inside of the quotidian of Life.

Your names have been picked out, dreamt of, and giddily decided,
By your mother and I, you could even say,
Before the beginning of time; well yours' anyway.

As such, I ask you to recall,
Being is Becoming is out-and-out an utter gift;
All the way down and all the way up.

Rufus Wingo Deyton

Rufus, Rue, Son.
You were the first we decided upon,
The first pang of anticipation we felt in our chests.
I do not know if you will be the first to arrive,
    or if you will come at all,
But I love the thought of a son whom I have invited to bear it all.

Your name means red-headed warrior.
Or, if we appeal to Mark (15:21),
You are the son of a burden-bearer;
And don't we both know that that is the truth?

Or, if we were to consult Paul (Romans 16:13),
I could call you chosen by our Lord;
But for what, for how, for why,
I do not yet know.

But this I do know:
I will bear your burdens,
I will wear your wounds,
I will hope your hopes,
And, I will dream your dreams.

Rufus, my red-headed warrior,
Seize this gift, bear the burden of hoping against hope,
And remember,
Your father would take up the suffering of a stranger,
There is no measure of what I will take up for you.

Charlotte Marie Deyton

Sun-pecked cheeks upon your mother's carbon–copy face.
Your joy is riveting in this world marked by so many hopeless imaginations.
Innocent and charitable, grace was gifted to you at birth,
Sainthood is of no effort for the cut of the cloth from which you are hemmed.

Daughter of mine, Charlotte, Charlee, your mother's delight,
There is no place, no, not height or depth,
That the ray of your beatific heart won't pierce and renew.

And on accounting for all this,
I am left breathless with a nagging question:
How am I, a spiteful, decrepit creature, pitiless, and wounded
To be the father of the heart of God?

Will you accept me, as your mother did,
Despite my edges, and callous heart,
Despite my hateful gaze and hard-fought, so-called wisdom,
Which only often leaves me feeling self-assured
And everything else around me at the edge of doubt and peril.

No, no you won't accept me . . .
You'll transfigure me.
For I will never know love like the kind which pours forth from your heart,
From your mind,

From your very soul.

You'll have your mother's everything, despite my failures.

Charlotte Marie,

One as our Blessed Mother Mary,

Your Fiat is always so eager.

May God's hand never leave you,

And, may you recklessly lead God by that hand,

As I imagine your curiosity, vitality, and imagination often compelling you to do for me,

To the ones who need Him most.

Edgar Byrd Deyton

It is a Tuesday and we are in a beige, humming waiting room.
Not long from now,
You will be a few teeth shorter,
And let's hope they take not their namesake from you,
Wisdom in this world is in short supply.

You don't know this,
Though I have warned you,
This operation can sneak up on you.
My own was particularly bad,
A dry socketed mouth and no pain medication;
Anyway, my memories aren't yours, so why would you trust them?

They take you back and then you arrive back on the scene.
Delirious, and puffy-faced,
I giggle to myself, but also know
That you are rubbing against your first take at suffering.

On the way home you ask for a milkshake,
I remind you of the rules about straws,
And you sigh.

We stop and get you vanilla ice cream to melt at home.
And I grab the malt powder because you love it like I do,
Despite your mother's silly opinion that it is 'odd-tasting.'
My son, your immaculate taste you inherit from me.
I smile, and remember that for a few days after,
You won't.

We arrive home and I medicate you.
You run off to sleep off your recent loss of wisdom,
Or your new-found wisdom, however, you want to read that.

It is 10 pm, and I hear you whimper and rattle about
As you grow in discontent.
I medicate you once more
And spend the rest of the night watching your TV,
Rubbing your back and smiling knowing you're safe
Because I am watching over you.

You don't know or notice my presence,
But that's not the point, is it?
Anyway, my memories aren't yours, so when you wake,
I'll just be Dad, and you'll just be Edgar Byrd.
But from one poet to another,
I'll always remember these moments most.

Saoirse Ruth Deyton

Well, here we are,
Last to currently be anticipated.
Saoirse Ruth, your name means freedom.

It is Irish, Celtic actually, and one day you will know
    just how Irish I am,
For I remember your little fingers wrapping and tugging at
    my bright red beard,
In the early morning hours, holding and rocking you beside your
    crib.
You always had to touch, to play, to grasp, to figure it out.

Ruth is a special homage in our family.
My great aunt, Ina Ruth, was the freest woman I've ever known,
Who chose not marriage, to settle, or to put up with
    the misfortune in life,
But instead, on her terms,
Opened a beauty shop that she owned, managed, and ran with
    vigorous energy.
Volunteered to raise even the most distant of cousin's children
    in that shop
(Counting these up,
I estimate some 49 children called Ina's shop home pre-school
    and during the summer),
And, still managed to be the most joyous and unbashful person
    in the room.

You see Saoirse,
We call you free,
We see how much you love beauty,
And above all,
How much you believe in justice,
In figuring it out on your own.

Saiorse Ruth,
A name meaning, for us at least,
To be responsible to and for freedom.

It is up to you to find out what that means,
I just hope you see how much your brother(s) and sister(s),
Your mother and father,
Your grandparents,
And most importantly,
The host of Heaven,
Support you.

You will change this world in only the way you can,
And I'll remind you, the world is both this house, this community, this patch of grass,
And Nations, Principalities, and Powers.
You are free, my daughter, my friend,
Act accordingly.

Jungle Gym Hands

The Sun is setting at the playground now,
You remember, the one behind the elementary school,
Across the street from the Presbyterian and Lutheran churches?

Anyways, you won't remember this moment,
Because you all are playing, seemingly, a game about pirates stealing treasure.
The girls are the merchants, the boys the pirates, it appears, but I am at a distance.
I watch, and smile, and remember, yet again, you are going to be people!

Involved in political decisions, in love, in violence.
You are the fabric of history.
And, you are . . . the kid who just faceplanted on the slide.
No history makers—yet.
Well, except you are.

I remember—I must have been 7 or 8, and it was during recess at school,
Playing a similar game of cops and robbers,
Or war,
Or something of the like,
And I was tasked with being a spy.

The other team had a base in a blue-tinted plastic slide,
But they didn't realize that the adjacent jungle gym provided a perfect eavesdropping perch.
So, naturally, I put this together and began my ascent.
One bar at a time, the jungle gym created an ascending half-sphere shape.
If one could make it up to the top, they could blend in pretty well with the rest of the climbers,
And yet, see everything on the battlefield.

On my way up,
My hands began to burn.
The sun was shining directly on the silver, exposed metal bars,
Creating a perfect hot iron for me to grasp at.

I didn't make it;
My hands were pretty burnt, and I fell.
The impact on my knees and the heat on my hands,
It all hurt so bad.
I tried and tried again, but I just couldn't make it.

Even now, as I whisk back to my body,
To my eyes and ears set upon you, my children,
I remember the pain, the embarrassment, the irritation
Of my jungle gym hands.

You are just children, but you aren't.
You are vulnerable,
You are playful,
You are me and I am you.

You make history, even if it is just your quiet, private,
    deep-down history,
And history has made us.
Especially that deep-down history.

And suddenly I realize,
Even though you aren't real yet,
You are the most really real thought I have had,
For every moment of my life, every experience,
Every jubilee and every storm,
All have been building blocks for the gift I hope to one day give you:

The gift of history, to have been and will be,
The chance to acquire your own hard-fought, exhausting,
    most meaningful
Jungle gym hands.

Grin

The playful pitter-patter plop of feet upon hardwood
Echoes through the kitchen of my mind.

And though you don't yet exist,
Your smile carves itself into me.
Like sunshine,
Cuts across the mantle above my blazing heart's open hearth.

A son, a daughter,
A chance to give myself for Life.
This call to love much, much more than,
Seizes me all the time.

And should you never grace a here or there, a now or then,
Just know within my heart of hearts,
I'll always be your friend.

And I hope and hope,
And hope again,
Everyday, to come to memorize your—
That lovely, all-consuming—
Mesmerizing, wonder-grasping grin.

To My Carlee (I'll Make the Toast)

I write to my Carlee,
Or your Matilda, or Johnathan, or who have you;
But I have a Carlee, and she has a me,
And so, I write to her, my dearest.

I am not quite sure how to tell the world how much I love you.
So maybe, this poem, this little slipping–spillage of ink onto a page,
Maybe this could be a quiet little corner for us to come
    and seek some shade,
And for us to whisper I love you in the way we would.

You can plant the Sugar Maples just over there,
Right beside the period, just up above.
Maybe your garden can go up by the word 'write;'
I'm not sure, you're better at things, and place, and space, anyway. . .

. . . And, no, you can't fix my toast this morning,
It's my fault it burnt,
And there's no worry anyhow.
I'm sorry I hurt, and sigh, and pout or pitter about from time to time.
But no, I'll make the toast.

www.ingramcontent.com/pod-product-compliance
Lightning Source LLC
Chambersburg PA
CBHW061249040426
42444CB00010B/2316